Contents

What is it like?

Streets can be:
- wide or narrow
- straight or curving
- busy or quiet
- new or old.

> • What differences are there between the streets in these two pictures?
>
> • Which of the streets would you most like to go to? Why?

Think of some words that describe the street you live in.

The buildings along
a street may be:

- shops
- workplaces
- places of entertainment
- places of worship
- homes.

- Why do you think that many homes are built in separate streets, away from shops and factories?
- What do you call the part of the street where people walk?
- What would you hear if you walked along the street below?

WHERE YOU LIVE
Notice the sounds of different streets, as well as the buildings and objects that you see there.

7

The main street

In the centre of most villages and towns, there is a main street. The buildings on the main street are places that many people visit.

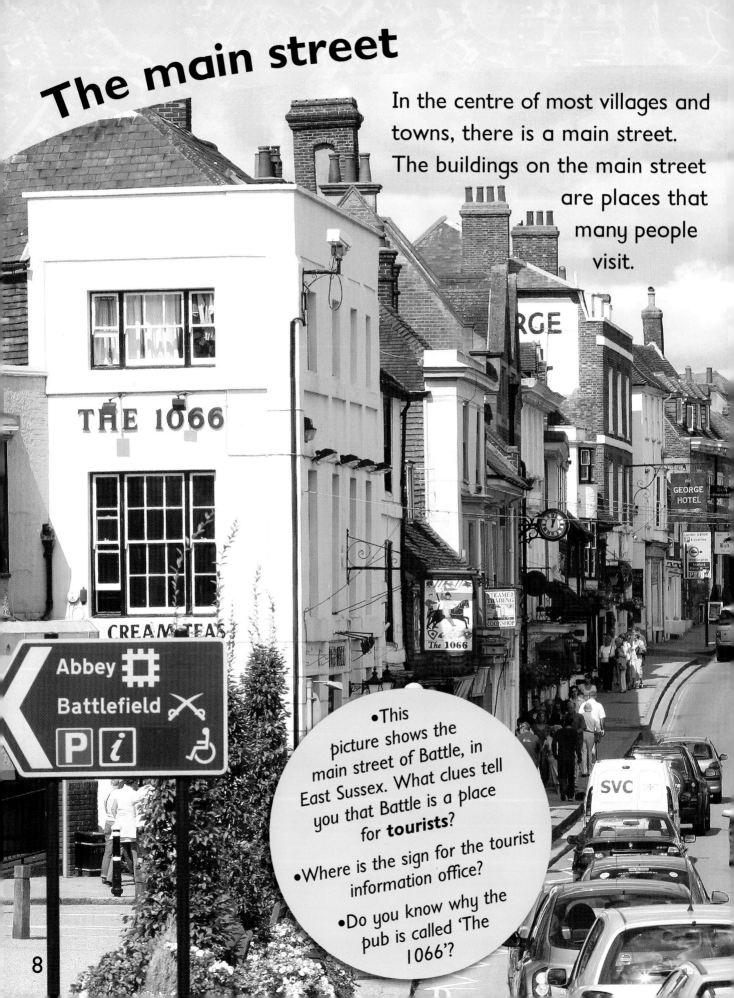

THE 1066

CREAM TEAS

Abbey
Battlefield
P i

GEORGE HOTEL

The 1066

STEAMER TRADING COOKSHOP

SVC

- This picture shows the main street of Battle, in East Sussex. What clues tell you that Battle is a place for **tourists**?

- Where is the sign for the tourist information office?

- Do you know why the pub is called 'The 1066'?

Sometimes the main street is called the **high street**. Streets that join up with the main street are called **side streets**.

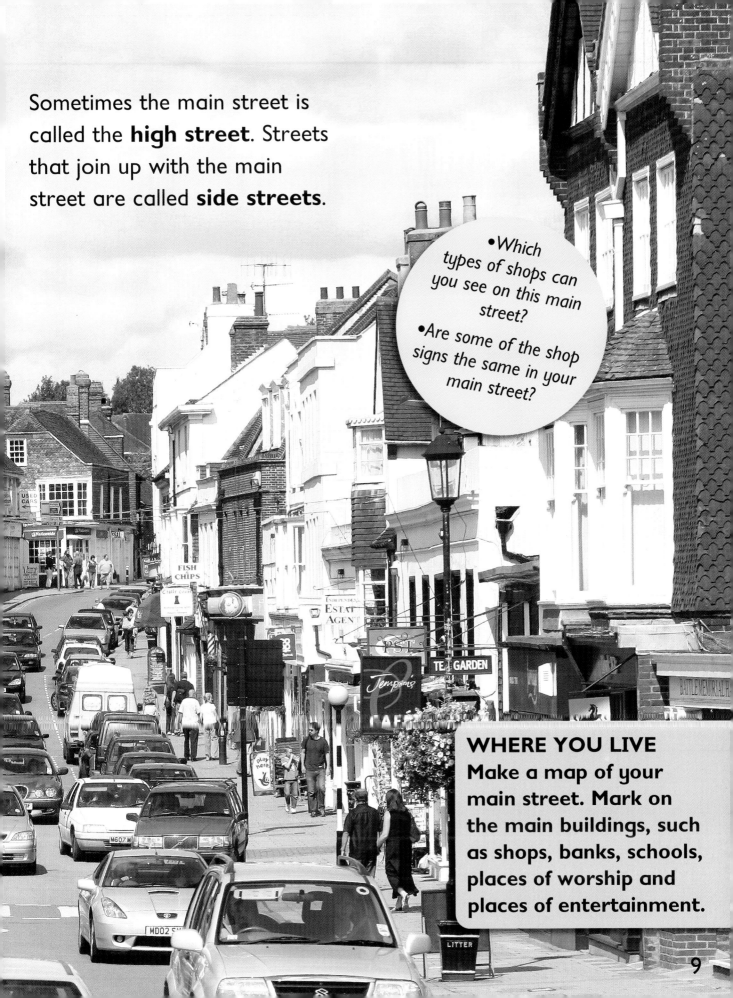

• Which types of shops can you see on this main street?

• Are some of the shop signs the same in your main street?

WHERE YOU LIVE
Make a map of your main street. Mark on the main buildings, such as shops, banks, schools, places of worship and places of entertainment.

Street shapes and names

A **through road** is a street that links two other streets.

Another type of street is called a 'dead end' or a **cul-de-sac**. Cars can drive into the road at one end, but there is no way through at the other end.

- Which through roads do you walk along on your way to school?

QUEBEC CLOSE

- Why do some people like to live in cul-de-sacs?
- How does the road sign tell you that Quebec Close is a cul-de-sac?
- Why do you think a cul-de-sac is often called a 'close'?

Some streets are named after places or people. The names may also tell you what the street is like. For example:
• An **alley** is very narrow.
• An **avenue** may be grand, with trees along it.

LAMB ALLEY

MAPLE ROAD LEADING TO PARK AVENUE

LUTON ROAD

• What does 'St' stand for?
• Which street is named after a queen of England?
• Where do you think Luton Road goes to?
• What work did blacksmiths do?

PARSONS HILL

BLACKSMITHS LANE

WHERE YOU LIVE
Look for street names, such as Blacksmiths Lane, that tell you about the work that people did there.

Traffic in the streets

The streets in some town centres are full of **traffic**.

•Which types of **motor vehicle** can you see in this street?

•How many traffic lights can you see?

Some drivers park and visit the town. Some drive through, on their way to another place.

Many signs, lights and markings on the road tell drivers and cyclists what to do and what not to do. Double yellow lines along the side of the road mean, 'No parking at any time.'

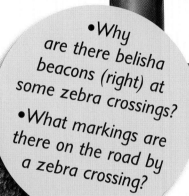

- What markings are there on the road outside your school?
- Why are there double yellow lines on the street below?

- Why are there belisha beacons (right) at some zebra crossings?
- What markings are there on the road by a zebra crossing?

- Why is traffic only allowed to go one way along some streets?
- What are speed bumps for?

One way

WHERE YOU LIVE
Find out what people think about problems caused by cars in the street where they live.

Walking in the street

People who walk in the street are called **pedestrians**. They should walk on the **pavement** to stay safe from traffic.

There are places to cross the street safely. An **underpass** (left) is like a tunnel under a street. The pedestrian crossing (below) is called a **puffin crossing**.

- What type of street has an underpass, for people to cross?
- What rules must you follow at a puffin crossing?
- Why is there a beeping sound when the green man shows?
- Which other types of crossing do you know?

In some towns, part of the main street is kept for pedestrians only. Can you think of the reason why pedestrian zones are good for pedestrians?

PEDESTRIAN ZONE
At any time
10am-6pm
At any time

WHERE YOU LIVE
Notice what pavements are made from. Which types of pavement do you like?

Under the street

Under the street are the pipes and **cables** that bring water, gas, electricity and telephone lines to our homes and other buildings.

WHERE YOU LIVE
Read signs that tell you about roadworks. Do they tell you what work is being done and how long it might take?

Water and gas workers can lift these covers in the pavement, to check the pipes.

- How many metal covers can you find in the street where you live?
- Have you seen rainwater rush down into a drain?

When it rains, water flows down the drain into an underground passageway called a sewer. Sewers carry away waste water from our buildings and streets.

Under some large, round covers in our streets there is a way down for workers who look after the sewers.

- Why do you think a cover like this is called a manhole cover?
- Can you find a manhole cover where you live?
- How does waste water travel away from your home?

Keeping the streets clean

Towns and villages are looked after by a **council**. One of the council's jobs is to make sure that rubbish is taken away or **recycled**.

• What do you do with rubbish at your home?
• Who comes to take it away?
• Does your council give people recycling boxes? What do you put in them?

People pay money to the council. The council uses the money to pay rubbish collectors and street cleaners.

St Albans
CITY AND DISTRICT

MAXIMUM PENALTY
£100

KEEP DOGS ON LEADS

MAXIMUM PENALTY
£100

CLEAN IT UP!

The council also makes rules, to help keep the streets clean and tidy.

In some places a notice says 'Please do not feed the pigeons. They make a mess and damage buildings.'

• Why do you think litter is left in some streets? Can you think of several reasons?

• What would you do to stop litter? Can you think of three suggestions?

WHERE YOU LIVE
What is the name of your council? Find out about the jobs it does to look after your town or village.

A good place to be

Many things make a street a good place for people to be.

It is good if there is plenty of space for people to move about.

• In these two pictures, what can you see that makes the street good to be in?
• Which things can block people's way on some pavements?
• What do you think is the best type of pavement for someone driving a **mobility scooter**?

It is good if there are places to sit and chat.

It is good if it is easy to find the places that you want.

Postboxes are easy to find, because they are always red and they show up clearly in the street.

It is good if police and other people are at work to make sure that the street is safe for everyone.

•What signposts are there for pedestrians in your town or village?

•What does **WC** stand for?

•What useful things are there behind the postbox in the picture?

WHERE YOU LIVE
Make a list of all the reasons why people visit your main street.

21

Looking up

When you explore the streets where you live, don't forget to look upwards.

- What does this lamp post have on it?
- Does your town have a badge, like the shield on this lamp post? What does your town badge look like?
- Why do we need street lamps?
- Which type of street lamp do you think looks best?

LCV ADVERTISER

10K
RUNNING FOR LIFE
Sunday 8th October
Rothamsted Experimental Station in Harpenden
Tel: 01727 731010
Email: tom@grove-house.org.uk
Web: www.grove-house.org.uk/herts10k

10K

LCV ADVERTISER

You can find some interesting things if you look up at buildings. The tops of shop buildings may be different from what you expect. This weather vane tells you which way the wind is blowing.

A camera may look down at you. It sends pictures to a control room, for people to check that there are no problems in the street.

WOOLWORTHS

Sup drug HEALTH&BEAUTY

WHERE YOU LIVE
Look for interesting buildings, like these above the shops, in your main street.

23

Decorating the streets

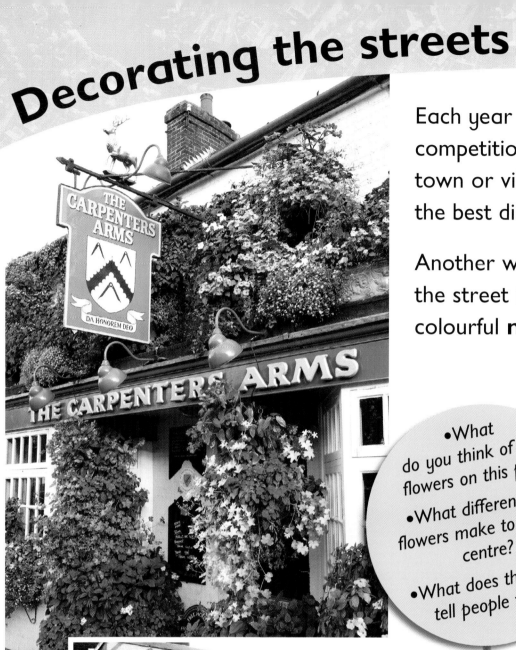

Each year there are competitions to see which town or village can make the best displays of flowers.

Another way to decorate the street is to paint a colourful **mural**.

- What do you think of the flowers on this pub?
- What difference do flowers make to a town centre?
- What does this mural tell people to do?

For **festivals**, people may decorate the street with flags or lots of lights.

- What festivals do people celebrate in your town or village?
- How do people decorate the streets for the festivals?
- When do you think the streets look the prettiest?

WHERE YOU LIVE
Visit a street that is decorated for a festival. What do you see, hear and feel?

How has the street changed?

The character of a street comes from:
- its buildings
- the surfaces of the road and pavements
- the street furniture, such as lamp posts
- the traffic and pedestrians who use the street.

100 years ago

The two pictures here show the same street at different times.

Look carefully at the pictures to find what has stayed the same and what has changed. Try to say why you think each change has happened.

- Why are there no cars in the picture on page 26?
- Why are there no cars in the picture below?
- What types of buildings are there in the street?
- When do you think the street looked nicest? What do you like about it?

Today

WHERE YOU LIVE
See if your library or local history archive has old photographs of your main street. What changes have taken place?

Glossary

Alley A very narrow street between buildings, usually for pedestrians only.

Avenue A wide, grand-looking street. Some avenues have a row of trees along each side. The word 'Avenue' is also used in the names of some streets that are not like this.

Cables Bundles of electrical wires, wrapped in a material that protects them.

Council A group of people who make decisions about how a town or village is run and organise things, such as schools, road repairs and rubbish collection, for all the people who live there.

Cul-de-sac A street that is closed at one end. It does not lead anywhere. 'Cul-de-sac' is French for 'bottom of a sack'.

Festivals Special times of year when people celebrate something that is important to them. Some festivals are to remember an important event in the history of a religion.

High street The main shopping street of a town.

Mobility scooter A battery-powered vehicle for someone who is not able to walk about easily in the street. The scooters can be used on the pavement.

Motor vehicle Any road vehicle that has an engine. Motor vehicles include cars, vans, motor bikes, buses and lorries.

Mural A large picture that is painted straight on to a wall.

Pavement An area along the side of a street that is only for the use of pedestrians and people with mobility scooters.

Pedestrians People who are walking about in a town or village. When you are a pedestrian, you can also say that you are getting about 'on foot'.

Puffin crossing A type of road crossing, where a pedestrian can push a button on a box by the side of the road and this tells the traffic lights to change so that the traffic will stop.

Recycled Used again. When rubbish is recycled, it is sometimes used again in a different way from before. For example, plastic bottles are made into a material that is used to make outdoor furniture.

Side street A street that you can turn into from the main street. Often side streets are smaller and narrower than the main street.

Through road A road that is open at both ends. It leads from one road to another.

Tourists People who visit a place for pleasure, for example on holiday or for a day out.

Traffic All the vehicles that use a street.

Underpass An underground passageway, by which pedestrians can cross from one side of a street to the other. An underpass is built where there is lots of traffic. This may be at a crossroads or where several wide streets cross each other.

WC Water Closet This was an old expression for a lavatory or toilet. Some signposts to toilets say 'Toilets', some say 'WCs' and some say 'Public Conveniences'.

Further information

To find out about the streets where you live, you need to do some field trips in your town or village and look at a street map and a large-scale Ordnance Survey map.

http://mapzone.ordnancesurvey.co.uk/
  is a fun site to learn about maps.

http://www.bbc.co.uk/england/webcams/
  Here you can see photos of places around Britain today.

You may find pictures of the streets in the past, in books at your local library, or by asking at your local studies archive or a local museum. These places may also have maps from the past. You can also find old maps at **http://www.old-maps.co.uk**.

There are some good websites where you can search for old photographs of some places, for example:

http://www.picturethepast.org.uk
  (for old pictures of Derbyshire and Nottinghamshire)

http://history.powys.org.uk/school1/ primhome.shtml
  (for material about Victorian mid-Wales)

http://www.staffspasttrack.org.uk/
  (for old pictures of Staffordshire)

http://gtj.org.uk
  (for old pictures of Wales)

To learn more about road safety, go to

http://www.thinkroadsafety.gov.uk/ arrivealive/index.htm

You can find out the name and details of your local council by going to

http://www.direct.gov.uk/Dl1/Directories /LocalCouncils/fs/en

Books

Exploring Seaside Towns, Katie Orchard, 2004 (Hodder Wayland)

Exploring Villages, Katie Orchard, 2004 (Hodder Wayland)

Earth in Danger: Settlements, Polly Goodman, 2001 (Hodder Wayland)

Earth in Danger: Transport, Polly Goodman, 2001 (Hodder Wayland)

Geography Detective Investigates: Your Local Area, Ruth Jenkins, 2006 (Hodder Wayland)

One World: In the City, Valerie Guin, 2007 (Franklin Watts)

One World: On the Move, Valerie Guin, 2007 (Franklin Watts)

One World: Where We Live, Valerie Guin, 2007 (Franklin Watts)

Safety First: On the Road, Ruth Thomson, 2004 (Franklin Watts)

Safety First: On Your Bike, Ruth Thomson, 2004 (Franklin Watts)

Start-Up Geography: Traffic and Safety, Anna Lee, 2006 (Evans Publishing)

Step-Up Geography: Should the high street be closed to traffic? Julia Roche, 2005 (Evans Publishing)

Step-Up Geography: Local traffic – an environmental issue, Anna Lee, 2006 (Evans Publishing)

Index